Ways to Make a Halo

Ways to Make a Halo

Poems by

Kevin Casey

Kelsay Books

ISBN: 13- 978-1-947465-29-9

Kelsay Books
Aldrich Press
www.kelsaybooks.com

Acknowledgments

Many thanks to the editors of the journals in which the poems below first appeared:

The High Window: "Botany Lesson"
Pennsylvania Literary Journal: "Spring Flower Arrangement," "Central Vacuum System," "A Soccer Ball in March," "Fable for a Wilderness Tamed"
Pamplemousse: "Allspice"
The Piedmont Journal of Poetry & Fiction: "A Haven of Rest and Order," "Agnus Dei," "Liner Notes to My Beatification"
Third Wednesday: "Revolving Door"
Lakeview Journal: "Typo in a Church Bulletin"
Sinkhole: "Food Poisoning," "Mondegreen"
Anti-Heroin Chic: "An Updated Constellation"
Apeiron: "At the Museum Giftshop"
London Journal of Fiction: "Man Drowns in Cruise Ship Pool"
Miller's Pond: "English as a Second Language"
The Mondegreen: "Street Sweeper"
Mud Season Review: "To an Air Raid Siren"
Lunch Ticket: "Timbre to Color"
Bluepepper: "Safety Razor"
Pinyon: "Sick at Christmas"
By & By: "To the Harpist in the Hospital Waiting Room"
Offcourse: "For an Arch Not Built," "Landscape with Pumpkins," "Quartering Downstream"
Transnational: "Eyeglasses"
Writer's Block Magazine: "Renovating the Bathroom," "Wishing Well"
Birch Gang Review: "Chase and Escape"
Roanoke Review: "An Adage"
Killing the Angel: "His Acre of Orchard"
Provo Canyon Review: "Fiddleheads," "Falling Asleep Deer Hunting"

Crack the Spine: "Suburban Choka No. 4"
Noble Gas Quarterly: "Border Town," "Musical Box"
Gravel: "Aiming Off"
Whistling Shade: "During a Midday Break from Hauling Wood"
Extract(s): "At the West End of Long Pond"
Suisun Valley Review: "An Antique Clock"
Picaroon: "Ways to Make a Halo"
Skylight 47: "Virga"
Dappled Things: "The Tarn"
Calamus Journal: "Blue Willow China in a Mountain Cabin"
Green Briar Review: "On the Discovery of Honey"
London Grip: "Snowstorm: For an Infant Son"
Boyne Berries: "Reading the Night Sky"

Contents

There are Moments

One

Two

There are Moments

when I could swear this will never end,
    when your laugh tumbles down like a brook

etched into a hillside: a necklace
    with a broken clasp, clear facets glittering

as they fall in the perfect luxury
    of a never-ending stream of moments.

One

Botany Lesson

I had grown a bean plant earlier that spring,
    sprouted on the kindergarten windowsill

in a towel-lined cup, so when my uncle warned
    that an orange seed washed down with my juice

would grow a tree inside of me, I pictured
    the buff pip cracked apart, blanched cotyledons

splitting somewhere within that wet darkness,
    the warm humus of organs clutched in a tracery

of rhizomes, a relentless taproot
    snaking down a leg toward the earth.

But in this misconception, a stark homily:
    the hardened rind that shields the seed,

our flesh that feeds what grows inside,
    lush and impatient, at last will give way

to a crown of leaves that erupts like wings
    and the nodding head of a blossom

that reaches toward the sun—then nothing
    but a fragrance and the memory of color.

Spring Flower Arrangement

The kitchen was steeped in its soapy
perfume until the peonies drooped
and a citrus smell emerged, verging
on vinegary. By the end of the day,
the scent had shifted to rain-soaked moss,
and then stale hops: an empty beer glass
in the morning sun. As the once-waxen
tulip petals grew set with a branching
filigree, their smooth magenta curled
in volutions of cream, fawn and ochre.
Such corrupt beauty blossoming, dappled
and urgent, like an argument to stay,
as I brushed the petals from the table,
and poured the clouded water down the sink.

Allspice

It stands on the shelf of the pantry,
shoulder to shoulder with the other
white canisters, sheepish and filled
with its brown-powdered shame:

in a glaring overreach of naming, it falls
far short of the needle-floored forest
evoked by rosemary, or the bite of dill
and mustard, and whatever purpose
somebody hoped that tumeric might fill.

Sage, for instance, seems to know its place,
that it's set aside almost solely for poultry,
as opposed to a spice someone named "all,"
which barely embodies "some," and in ways
is little more than a synonym for "cinnamon."

A Haven of Rest and Order

A found poem, comprised entirely of lines from the Minnesota
Multiphasic Personality Inventory-2 (a common test for adult
psychopathy), and a 1955 article in Housekeeping Monthly.

Often I get confused and forget what I want to say. *This is a way of
letting him know that you are concerned about his needs.*

Lately I have lost my desire to work out my problems. *Touch up
your make-up, put a ribbon in your hair and be fresh-looking.*

I have very few quarrels with members of my family. *Clear away
the clutter: Don't ask him questions about his actions or question*

*his judgment or integrity. Don't greet him with complaints and
problems. Minimize all noise.* I often feel as if things are not real.

At times I think I am no good at all. *Let him talk first - remember
his topics of conversation are more important than yours.*

Once in a while I feel hate toward members of my family whom I
usually love. *Prepare the children.* I am made nervous by certain

animals. *Speak in a low, soothing and pleasant voice. You have no
right to question him.* The things that some of my family have

done have frightened me. *After all, catering for his comfort will
provide you with immense personal satisfaction.* When a man is

with a woman he is usually thinking about things related to her
sex. *Be a little gay and a little more interesting for him. His boring*

day may need a lift. I can't go into a dark room alone, even in my
own home. *Make the evening his. Make him comfortable.*

One or more members of my family are very nervous. *They are little treasures and he would like to see them playing the part.*

Some of my family members have quick tempers. *Try to understand his world of strain and pressure and his very real need*

to be at home and relax. Terrible thoughts about my family come to me at times. *Be happy to see him. Never complain. A good wife*

always knows her place. The man should be the head of the family. Many people treat me more like a child than a grown-up.

Try to make sure your home is a place of peace and tranquility. I almost never dream.

Central Vacuum System

The last house we all lived in together,
    before the apartments, was plumbed throughout
        with off-white tubes leading from knee-high holes

that pocked the fake wood paneling
    and avocado paint in every room.
        With the flip of a switch the house would hum,

and—Tareyton dangling—my mother
    would make short work of the dog hair
        on the deep-piled rug of burnt orange,

and the crumbs that littered the corners
    of the kitchen's harvest gold vinyl.
        But with each passing year, the pull

of another room's socket would weaken,
    then fail. Blame would collect with the dust:
        the children who must have clogged it with toys,

our father too harried to fix the issue,
    our mother who resented a portable
        workaround out of principle.

There were a few good years when everything
    worked, and the motor hidden in the heart
        of the basement kept us neat and efficient.

Then one by one, the dark inlets were doused
    like stars, the plastic framework failed, and the whole
        constellation was finally extinguished.

Revolving Door

I stepped onto the platform in a city
    at the end of its Art Deco morning,

holding my grandmother's white-gloved hand
    in crosswalks between the curved flourishes

of tailfins on Chryslers, car horns echoing
    off the skyscrapers' glass and concrete walls.

The horizon lay hidden, exchanged
    for patterns of opulent sunbursts

and chevrons carved in low-relief onto friezes
    that raced adjacent boulevards within

a streamlined metropolis rushing
    to the end of its post-war trajectory.

Once coaxed to let go of her hand and step
    into the spinning contraption standing

guard at the department store, I rode
    its fluttering brass wings counterclockwise

until my grandmother lost patience—
    going nowhere in the turning whirligig,

twirling, enchanted, with all the wedges
    and wing-tips, both motion and purpose

there and all throughout the city limits
    now little more than glorious ornament.

Agnus Dei

We watched his grandchildren play
most weekends from our stunted porch,
between the balusters and passing cars,
through bus exhaust and construction sounds.

They called him *Papou* as they hung
on the old man's neck—our neighbor,
but a world away across that treacherous street.

Each Easter, we would wake to see a lamb
hanging in his crooked garage—its soft,
stretched body as white as the rope that fastened it,
and that tragic cerise slit that split its frame.

And each Easter we thought, what a shame
that such a beautiful thing had wandered
lost into our city to meet such a pointless end;
what a sad sacrifice to carelessness.

Typo in a Church Bulletin

The inerrant word of God inclined
    in the rack on the pew-back in front of me,

but as the scripture lesson began
    I chose instead to read the church bulletin.

And having found a spelling error
    on the second page, I was divided

as to whether I should feel pity
    for the poor church secretary, pride

at my cleverness, or guilt for my gloating.
    By the time the organ announced the next hymn,

I had closed the bulletin to admire
    the sweep of the painted dove's wing featured

on the cover, resolving that the day's
    catechism should instead take its cue

from the light that dyed the pamphlet in my hand,
    filtering through the colored panes in hues

that both contrasted and yet were fused,
    the morning and myself disregarding

the soldered stories of whatever figures
    were stained upon that wall of windows.

Food Poisoning

Flat on the bathroom floor at 2 a.m.—
eyes open, and the porcelain font
loomed above me like a ghastly chalice.
Eyes closed, I had visions of Saint Anthony
torn by demons in a tile-lined cave.

Thirty pieces of silver for that salad,
that unholy host, then wretched and retching—
betrayed by my whole body, my mind
seething in a sour martyrdom.

No recollection of a state before
this suffering, and no faith that grace
might save me, I ached to understand my sin,
to know what had left me so forsaken.

But once the daylight shivered across the sill,
there was only one revelation I took
from that floor: if the Bridegroom had come
for me that night, I would have gladly taken
his hand, and placed it against my fevered cheek.

An Updated Constellation

It's a pearlescent scribble I've traced for myself:
    affixed within its net are caught a thousand stars.

And while this luminous stain assumes far more
    than its share of night, and of my day, it resists

all augury, knows nothing of the future, denies
    any notion of destiny or fate. Instead, it casts

a backward glance along the lonely zodiac—
    outlining loss and flaws, it maps a wistful path

toward regret, glowing in celestial
    self-reproach as its declination diminishes.

At the Museum Gift Shop

I hold a lump of amber to the skylight,
and the glossy, pumpkin knuckle is a prism
in reverse, absorbing fractured light,
compressing it to saffron smoldering.

But pivoting my wrist to catch the facets
etched among the bits of ancient insects
I can't recall the card from the display
I'd read not twenty minutes past—

how long ago did the giant fern-tree weep
that shed this burnished tear? A million years?
One hundred? It seems something I should know...

Surface-stuck on these fly-paper days,
I can't discern a decade through this lens
of frozen honey, let alone some unreal millions.

And so back into the bin it goes, silent,
its mythical depths still unsounded—
just another pretty, semi-precious gem.

Man Drowns in Cruise Ship Pool

The rich and krill-thick brine that rinses
the lungs' pink coral, and the light shafts
piercing the pearls of breath that rise
in spirals toward the mottled sun—

O, there's forty fathom or more below,
no danger there from wreck nor gale
amidst the veils of kelp. But you weren't
wrapped in an oil-skin and jumper, a clewline
trailing from your hand as you sank away
back into the arms of the cold Atlantic,
ruing this life's brief shore leave,
to live your death among the horned wrack
and sand sharks that prowl
the channel to St. George's port.

Denied that secret of the mariner's dream,
you bob back to the surface of a bright,
tiled pool, through the thin film of chlorine
that foams about your limbs as you're pulled
into the shallow end, your fellow passengers
horrified and leering, deck chairs scattered.

Still, high above, a gull rides the following wind
to guide you back north, the rudder swung hard over,
past the light that guards the ledges off Cohasset.

English as a Second Language

The first couple of years after college,
the difficult part wasn't enduring
that same diet of noodles and chicken franks
cooked in a kitchenette with thrift store pans
in the gray exile of a new city,

cashing in early on weekend nights,
walking home along the broken asphalt
between the bleared halos of shop lights
from a slightly higher than minimum-wage job
teaching English as a Second Language.

Instead, it was the missing gallery
of faces—supportive, disappointed,
but always mindful. All those watchful eyes
that seemed to care if I succeeded or failed
had faded, turned away to their own worries

and concerns, the assembly now replaced
with the earnest faces of a dozen
young Korean women to whom I taught
idioms and clauses two nights a week,
their gaze rarely lifted higher than their desks.

And when I asked them before our first test
if there were any lingering questions,
they were all too mortified to confess
and to accuse, to reveal that our weeks
in the classroom had all been in vain,

and so each one would fail. But that evening
they shook their raven heads and lied to one

of the faces lined up to judge their lives,
this one behind a lectern, saying:
No, thank you. We are OK, Mr. Sir Casey.

Street Sweeper

Fairfield Street, Boston, 2003

Backed into their corrugated caves, the plow trucks
　　hibernate, and now the street sweeper has returned

from its slow migration, crawling like a marigold snail
　　beneath my half-opened sash. When winter had grown

out of its charm, its midnight storms magnified
　　our isolation, and we waited for the rumbling

scythe to glide through the boulevard, its low lullabye
　　echoing along the brownstones, clearing away

the burden of our separate solitudes. The sand
　　it scattered never seemed to measure up to much

until the rains came, and the storm drains grew choked
　　with rivers of silt. Inside, little changed with the seasons—

the tilt of morning light across the paths we wore
　　throughout these rooms, the tapping of the radiator's

cryptic code grown fitful, then silent. You left to make
　　your own way long before the sweeper returned,
　　　　tracing waves of scoured pavement in its wake.

Liner Notes to My Beatification

Resplendent in this monstrance
of silver-gilt and crystal,
I await requests for intercession,
standing on the subway platform—
my concrete hermitage.

O charism, fugitive charism—
the train has pulled away
with my communicants, and I'm left
spinning, solitary in the rumbling

of its sedulous wake,
grasping for grace—some gift,
some token from without
to complete this canonization.

O charism that makes pigs to see
the wind—where is the tangled script
that I might speak in tongues,
a sunbeam to hang my washing on,
that would sanction my veneration?

To an Air Raid Siren

Long after they set you upon your roost
    atop the armory to warn of bombers

that might come streaming up the valley
    thick as autumn starlings, and once your watch

for the atom flash that would swallow the sun
    and set fire to shadows was over,

the town fathers voted to keep you perched
    overlooking the schools and churches,

shops and factories, to hit and hold
    your lunch-time note. And when you sing each noon,

preening rust-streaked feathers, obliging
    their nostalgia for an antique terror,

are you keening for the loss of those
    who marched from this valley, never to return,

or are you calling out in loneliness
    now that the flocks of carrion birds

have flown in all directions to scour
    other valleys in their endless migration?

Timbre to Color

Today I have at last perfectly matched 'v' with "Rose Quartz"
in Maerz and Paul's Dictionary of Color.
—Vladimir Nabokov

"Azure" leaves the mouth thrumming on the tongue
like a tooth-trapped hummingbird—
the iridescence of a fly rattling in a web.

The acrid chartreuse scent of tansy belies
its yolky glow, while the strokes
and curls of its name evoke
the taut, smoky skin of an aubergine.

A matchstick flaring has a fine-grained,
saffron edge that abrades against stillness,
then abates to a lambent sigh.

And the mottled sky is steadied
by the weight of these wave-tossed cobbles,
heeled into a sea as smooth as a herring gull bone,
bleached and salt wind-burnished.

Safety Razor

I'm still enamored with the idea of it:
that an antique safety razor—sporting
a fresh leaf of steel—might in the end
be more scrupulous than those newfangled
plastic affairs, that this metal contraption
could show these disposable days just how
a man of quality and character shaves.

But each time I try to accompany those ranks
of no-nonsense men marching back into
the 19th Century with their Barbasol
and badger bristles, my cheeks end up
a red deeper than shame could ever muster,
my jawline left a half-stubbled field too steep
and cragged for a horse-drawn mower to manage.

Still, every few months I take down one of these
eleven-dollar thrift store beauties
from its glass-doored bathroom shrine
and hold its golden brass to my chin
like a buttercup, risk rashes and nicks
to see if I've grown worthy enough
to join that group of well-groomed ghosts
staring back just beyond the mirror's edge
through a mist of bay rum and witch hazel.

Sick at Christmas

At my sister's for the holidays, I packed
my head cold along with the bow-tied boxes
for her boys. Red-nosed and sneezing,

I was excused from a gathering
across town, allowed to stay behind—
an extra afghan placed upon me,

carols on the radio and colored lights
dappling the darkened ceiling, tucked in
with tissues on her guest room sofa.

Soon they'd return with leftovers, laughing
and banging snow from their boots in the mudroom,
but for now I haunted her house—a ghost

of Christmas past, somewhere between carefree,
cared for, and serene in that solitude:
a boy again in the convalescence of youth,

sent upstairs to bed Christmas eve,
falling asleep with my anticipation
to the warm tones of grown-ups reveling below.

To the Harpist in the Hospital Waiting Room

Wrinkled cherub with your cherrywood harp,
you've subdued the bustle of this room,
eased the commotion of nurse and needle,
tourniquet and gurney. The best of us
just bored, the worse off cradling arms

like infants or pressing gauze to our heads
as if lost in contemplation, we'll grant
you've elevated this space to something grand,
eternal, orchestrated a quaint limbo
from these rows of chairs and magazine racks.

But we're here to be assured we'll remain
tethered to our time, not to endure
this dour liturgy. We strain to hear
our names called, and someone with a clipboard
ask *now what seems to be the problem?*

Mondegreen

You'll likely have your own list of these:
misheard lyrics amusing to recollect
and share with feigned shame, once the pop tunes
of life's soundtrack subside to the stodgy
opera of adulthood, and you hum along
to the baffling language of grown-ups,
your voice settling into its lower register.

But you keep to yourself each lapse as you learn
the words to your middle life arias—the noble
vocation revealed as just another job,
the stranger's face mistaken for a soulmate.
And still you sing, sure of each verse
in the shower, belting out a bravura piece
in the car with the windows down,
the landscape in your wake littered
with pages of that mangled libretto.

For an Arch Not Built

We have taken it for granted that the Greeks were ignorant of the properties of the arch.
—Arthur Ashpitel, *Treatise on Architecture*, 1867

It's not that they weren't able to conceive
of such a thing, that neither the round
keystone of sun supporting the noon sky
nor the philtrum's wedge carved into the apex
of marble lips that carried so much weight
of expression never suggested the form.
Instead, it was just the difference
between desire and necessity
that guides even civilizations,
between the impulses of inertia
and inspiration—the bracing, time
and scaffolding required to stay with you,
for example, or leaving an enduring
"we" as just a theoretical construct.

Runway Reverie

The redeye rumbled around the tarmac
for so long that—drifting off—I dreamt
I was leaning against the window
of a bus, heading south again on 40

to the suburbs of Raleigh to propose
to my girlfriend, and leave her family
stirred and swirling in a turbulence
I rode like a tailwind back to NC State.

Jolted awake, it was a decade later—
the dream dissolved to lingering faces,
puzzled and fading in the port wing's light
as the plane escaped into the empty air.

Eyeglasses

Half a mask that whets
the dull facts of line and form,
these glasses gloss over

tone and hue, value and shade,
sharpening only edge and shape
into a surfeit of clarity.

Beyond this lens
and plastic sluice,
on the periphery

of its arcane cantilevers,
a blurred world seeps in—
a vaporous haze

that insinuates
a richer view.
The contraption folded away

at day's end, collapsed
on careworn hinges,
the near at hand

flows back into focus,
the mind reaching out
to reclaim depth and texture—

the visible grows
more bodily, and we see
into the life of things.

Renovating the Bathroom

It began before we signed the paperwork;
before we committed to buying the house
we knew the old tub surround would have to go,
and the pedestal sink whose drain was collared
with a blossom of verdigris and rust.

Condensation that dripped from porcelain
colluded with copper leaks and wet feet
to weep dampness beneath the vinyl floor,
staining and softening the boards beneath,
revealed when viewed from the cellar below.

And for years we did nothing but delay
and deny, until that spring when you began
spending nights on the sofa, and we sensed
something desperate needed to be done.

Then the plans came easy, and the choices
we made: the clawfoot tub from the catalog,
the new vanity we stored in the parlor
waiting for the plumbing to be prepared—
though we stopped agreeing about all else,
and our words were like sledges and pry bars
that demolished even civility in the end.

Despite all that damage, the negligence
and wreckage we fashioned within our house,
by the time autumn came and I agreed
to leave, we had rehabilitated
that room, satisfying some misplaced urge
within us both to fix and to make new.

Two

Chase and Escape

For love or anger, through hate or desire,
one red squirrel pursues another: a ribbon
of cinnamon wrapped in endless loops
about the trunk of the ashleaf maple,
defying the sights of my pellet gun,
confounding the windage and elevation
of the barrel resting on the porch rail.
That I might wind my way around each day
unscathed, knit within that same frenzied
blessing of chase and escape, braided
safely in that frenetic state of grace.

An Adage

When hornets' nests are hanging low
The winter will be light of snow.
—Anonymous

It hangs upon an alder branch,
a paper pendant in layered veins
of smoke and taupe, swaying at the edge
of an Indian Summer day.

This close to the ground, it seems
an argent emblem to us,
who would draw even the least
pitiless beast into our histories
and prophecies, would ask
a silent hive gravid with apathy
how deep the snow might fall.

And yet, so little interest
in the adage where the workers
starve before the first flake lands,
and the queen alone evades the frost,
concealed in a fold of hickory bark,
beyond the reach of ice or wind,
past any need of hope or knowing.

His Acre of Orchard

March is a winter month here, and again
my neighbor to the south labors through the snow,
loppers folded in the crook of his arm,
his round-runged ladder tracing a furrow
in the snow behind. Watersprouts and suckers

are splayed like whiskers about the foot
of every tree as he works his way across
his acre of orchard, and the cut ends
of what new growth the winter has managed
are left weeping sap between scales of bark.

Watching from my wood stove, his industry
seems reckless to one reluctant even
to presume that spring would come, yet somehow
from his ladder he sees beyond the cold,
past summer to another year's harvest.

A Soccer Ball in March

A week of early heat and the landscape's
    only white now glows from the soccer ball

tucked beneath the laurels, the wind spilling in
    from the south lifting the leaves of its nest.

It glows in the dusk like a candle, a dim
    and solitary remainder of luminous,

snow-blue evenings and featureless fields,
    moon-infused, at once effaced yet whole.

The scent of wet earth returns, and the sound
    of stream water on that same south wind

that flows around the ball—a glossy pearl
    within a dark and roughened setting,

now that winter has gone, and all the world
    has been laid bare and torn to fragments.

Fiddleheads

These jade snakes rear up each spring by the stream
    that coils itself about the hollow's floor.

Breaking through silt-matted leaves, they're crowned
    in bits of shell—paper scales torn from the hull of winter.

From each hydra nest, you'll cut a few heads
    throughout a quarter acre, then steal past

tongues of melt-water tumbling over
    sandstone lips, then up the embankment

with spring's first hatchlings swinging in your bucket
    to the sun on the road, and the hollow filled
        with the hissing of the stream behind you.

Suburban Choka No. 4

I'd wrench free the blade
from the mouth of this mower,
let the grass cascade
in waves that crest into seed,
if I might still sail
within the shores of my lawn—
my propellerless
vessel plying back and forth,
pressing out ripples
with its wheels in even rows
that echo through fall's stillness.

Window Weights

These iron ingots
stand listing,
staring skyward
at the small light
winking through
the pulley's groove—
ropes cut, sashes
painted shut,
tall buckets sunk
to the bottoms
of their wells,
and no help now
in drawing up
a summer breeze.

Border Town

So little room between the mountains
and the sky, along this high margin
of the empire, where layers of isolation
fold upon themselves, overlap like petals
tucked into the bud of a frostbitten flower.

All the tall pines were cut for masts
that sailed away a hundred year ago.
And buried beneath eight months
of snow, these hardscrabble fields yield
little but crops of drunks and martyrs.

But which of these children of pioneers,
abandoned in this town among the tote roads
and tin roofs, might imagine another way,
might choose to follow those gentle streams
to rivers that rush toward distant valleys,

and leave behind the aurora's quilling
and the balsam poplar's perfume,
might renounce their sole inheritance
and forsake all that desperate beauty?

Musical Box

After the Great War, Silas Talbot
had the men from Skowhegan run a few strands
of copper wrapped in tar tape through the silt
at the bottom of Long Pond, three miles to where
he worked in the woods with his wife. For years
the thin amber note of their gas light was lost
in the gulf of night, blue waves of snow
deadening the hum of their small cabin.

But once their telephone was installed,
it was only weeks before his wife
turned her mind to the upright piano
Silas had carted in years earlier,
to keep her occupied so far from town.

And for years afterwards, half the village
would call in to the party line on Friday
and Saturday evenings to hear her play
for an hour after dinner, wearing
her Sunday finery—flared Bakelite bells
resting on tables up and down main street,
and all the valley a musical box
ringing beneath its lid of quartz and sable.

Wishing Well

He had thrown in his lot with the weather
and the seasons, having been lucky enough
to come back in one piece from the war.
After two good harvests, there was money
to take a practical wife, and to bring
the well-digger to rattle his rig
through the shale at the end of the porch.
The young farmer turned a lucky penny
in his pocket, hoping water would be found,
while his practical wife stood in the doorway,
dishwater drying on her apron.

The pump in place and the house plumbed through—
all copper elbows and chrome spigots—
she made him buy a five dollar wishing well
at the hardware store to cover the stub
of steel casing now sprouting in her dooryard.
That miniature well with its shingled roof
was the sole metaphoric reach she would make
in all their married years, and if it was
just a rare decorative touch, or was made
to honor or deride his carefree nature,
in sixty years, he never thought to ask.

Aiming Off

Walking pathless among the swamp birch
at the eastern end of the pond, I'll emerge
to find a line of mountains waiting
across the white caps, and a wind pacing
the shore, glad to give me its accounting.

But still in the confines of these woods I hold
this compass rose before me like a suitor,
anxious to find the patient inlet stream
that opens to the waves and to the sun
that mottles the morning forest floor.

The needle knows just minutes and degrees
and nothing of the stream I'm seeking,
where water cooled by recent rains calls trout
from the pond's deep holes with its song of moss
and foaming falls. And so I'm aiming off,

targeting the shore far north of where
I wish to be, to guarantee the stream
will appear at some point on my southern way—
trading time for a surety of space,
while the sun slides along its westerly track,

and the stream falls within its ancient banks
and the wind still races everywhere,
as if there were some date it had to keep.

During a Midday Break from Hauling Wood

This camp was moved here eighty years ago,
along the road that follows the river,
by horses dragging it on skids over
snow, through town, then to this side of the pond.
Along the shore, children swing minnow nets,
stalking frogs among the shelves of dark shale.
The wind throws a diamond net over the pond,
and the boats begin to creak against the
grey dock. On the other side of the cove,
pine logs snap in a campfire, lit for lunch;
a loon calls out to warn that the eagle's
left the pine overlooking the river,
falling back toward the wild rice, endlessly.

At the West End of Long Pond

Rocking gently by the crib, the anchor
paid out just a few feet across the rocks
heaped up inside the old log frame submerged
beneath the pond, the May morning drifts by.

A half mile out, by the river's inlet,
the giant granite rock still keeps its watch
over the moose that come and go, feeding
on water grass in the shallows. Crowned with

stunted cedar and sheep laurel, its lag
ring rusts, that used to tie to this piling
and catch the logs in the spring drives as they
shoved and rolled their way downstream, knocking and

bobbing in the frozen, foaming water.
But the drives are gone now, given over
to trucks and skidders that comb the dark woods,
though the sun and waves still wash against these rocks.

Fable for a Wilderness Tamed

We moved into the cottage
beside the forest,
with a small wedge of lawn
and its slender lilac
holding fists of purple
against a wall of black spruce.

At first the snowshoe hares
would come at twilight—
furtive and variegated,
loping toward the torn bread
we'd throw, with the thrush
singing vespers from the night
that grew in the nearby woods.

But then it was the fox
that poured from the brake
like rust and fire,
with ivory for its bib,
and ivory at its brush's tip,
and the hares never returned.

Now each day the fox
waits for our dinner scraps,
and the mice from our traps,
and the three of us pay
little mind to the jay
that scolds from the night
in the nearby woods.

An Antique Clock

In the antique store, an open box hangs
on a bend of wire—thin boards as soft and dark
as charcoal from the slow fire of years,
and three gears fixed, run through by a spindle.

Among the shop's dowdy relics, fussy
in their clutter, the gutted clock quails,
conspicuous in the cruelty it's endured—
effaced, hands lopped off, and nothing left

of its pendulum except for the space
where it once paced—more a burglar-rifled
drawer than a device once precise
enough that it might have seemed mindful.

But time sees a mirror in every clock,
and—ever-grieving for the passing
of each dying moment—who could blame
time for singling out for destruction

a reflection that shows its haggard face
in mourning, for consuming in its flames
that scrupulous reminder of its anguish,
for silencing that endless, ticking requiem?

Ways to Make a Halo

Spin a broom at the sky to catch the flight
    of swifts in loops of liquid silver.

Hammer out a pewter ring from a length
    of smoke escaping a morning bonfire,
        using a sunbeam as an anvil.

Steal the twenty-seventh year growth ring
    from a lightning-struck sycamore tree.

Having pulled the darkness from a hole
    four feet deep, cut off the very bottom
        and roll up the sides to form a hoop.

Pare the rind of a manhole cover, then
    seal the ends with a paste of dew and pollen.

With the whittled end of a cattail stem,
    lift a ripple from an autumn pond
        the night before its surface slows to ice.

Virga

Common enough, and a phenomenon
hard to miss: a rain cloud gliding along
the horizon like a man o' war,
dragging damp tendrils that float above the ground.
But the term "virga"—the word for rain
that doesn't reach the earth—has no currency,
an inside joke too obscure to use
without a footnote. Though a metaphor
filled to bursting with parallels for missed marks,
for the incomplete and efforts wasted,
it's left to hang and dry upon its vine,
untapped and fated to remain little more
than a feathery crossword riddle—
five letters down, but not quite all the way.

Landscape with Pumpkins

Only a fragment of the rainbow showed,
its tag end heeled into the horizon
across the valley. Its blue matched the shade
that outlined the clouds, and what leaves were left
at the bottom of the field accented
the orange band in that partial arch,
and picked out the few wrinkled pumpkins left
along the fence by the shuttered farm stand.

There's little majesty in the landscapes
in this part of the world, only windbreaks
that tilt toward sluggish streams, tumbling
lines of stone walls and windrows—these vignettes
now washed with a patina like old varnish,
colors fugitive with the fading of the year.

But like a radiant gilt frame that borders
a darkened painting crazed and dimmed with age,
the cars parked along the lane—a dozen drivers
pulled over on their evening commute
to snap cell phone photos of this view—
outshone the humble grandeur of the scene
they stopped to see, the tableau they formed
in their shared impulse more vivid than that vista.

The Tarn

Wrenched from the granite and wind-bent,
the stunted spruce and red pine
fail at last to moss and reindeer lichen
near the summit's arch.

And set amidst their greenish-blue, it lies
a smooth jewel, enfolded
in the clear fire of wind forever
raging at this height.

Whether a facet fallen from the azure above,
or a glass fashioned and lifted
by the earth, held closer to heaven
in this mountain's grasp,

we have both come to this height
to make the sky know of its beauty.

Blue Willow China in a Mountain Cabin

I.
In exile among the black spruce,
this stack of antique plates forms
a half-rhyme of hue and shape
with the autumn sky and the circuit
of the moon. Fragile and luminous,
in all other aspects they rest distinct
within the orbit of their range
that rings the mountain's base.

II.
These vignettes of cobalt show
three figures robed, pagodas,
and two birds aspectant,
suspended in a crazed web of worn
glazing so unlike the pairs of mated jays
that decorate these darkened boughs;
and the willows here are of a strain
that have no weeping habit.

III.
Shelved upon this high meadow,
they sit within their lacquered cabinet,
each plate an island in a sea
of cold shadow, patens both
abandoned and abiding
in a hard-hewn tabernacle,
brought with care to this elevation,
for some unknown communion.

On the Discovery of Honey

An infant would put the sun in its mouth
if it could: the jangling bronze of dawn
overwhelming its curiosity,
and eyes too clouded, hands still too weak
to help it understand this new life.

But in the world's infancy, crawling
out of Eden with the taste of shame
still on our lips, it was hunger, not wonder
that drove us toward the humming combs—
reckless in our desperation, reaching
on tiptoe along starvation's edge
through the blear of searing barbs
to gnash fistfuls of summer sun.

Snowstorm: For an Infant Son

The headlights make a million threads
    of the falling snow, and the wind is a loom

that weaves them into a white cocoon
    surrounding my car, and at every curve

and downhill slope, I feel my rear wheels hold
    their breath as they lose contact with the road.

But it's the thought of you, at home and wrapped
    in your own cocoon of robin's egg flannel,

grown and driving through the weather of the world
    that I worry over, and not myself.

In you, there is no immortality,
    only a shift in that burden of care,

and with each mile into the blinding white
    I grow less significant,
        and my hands relax upon the wheel.

Quartering Downstream

The wind that nods the shocks of cotton grass
lavishes us in forgetfulness.
Noon sun that ponders over alder leaves
fashions a honeyed absence beneath,
dappling us inside an easy shade.

The pock and ripple that carve the flowing jade
from within, and the following urgence
trembling from leader to rod tip,
from sinew then deep into our marrow
affirms the illusion that another,
separate life might ply this same stream.

Falling Asleep Deer Hunting

A half-mile behind your house, bundled up
and boots crossed, your back tucked into the fold
of an ash tree, and the day creeps away
behind the sound of distant cars. A brief
dream follows, less strange than the waking—
dew on your coat, your nose numb with cold,
a rifle barrel heavy on your shin.
Buried in dusk, longing for neither home
nor solitude, you rise, shuffling through
leaves toward the smell of wood smoke, your compass
wheeling in the night that fills your pocket.

Reading the Night Sky

When night will pare away
the landscape from these windows,
and the day fall, folding like
a June bug's wing, you'll pass
the screen door, dooryard,
leave the porch light's orbit

toward the house's north,
and standing with the apple trees,
draw your mind along
the constellations' braille
to read the gauze
of guttering lights,
that lustrous web.

The frail flecks connect,
then disengage and shift—
shapeless, unfocused—
fragments churned in whorls,
dispersing to forgetfulness
at the rib of moon rising.

About the Author

Kevin Casey is the author of *And Waking . . .* (Bottom Dog Press, 2016), and American Lotus (Glass Lyre Press), winner of the Kithara Prize. His poems have appeared recently or are forthcoming in Rust+Moth, Valparaiso Poetry Review, Connotations Press, Pretty Owl Poetry, and Ted Kooser's syndicated column 'American Life in Poetry.' For more, visit: *andwaking.com.*

www.ingramcontent.com/pod-product-compliance
Lightning Source LLC
LaVergne TN
LVHW051607080426
835510LV00020B/3172